Authentic Traditional Memphis, Tennessee Recipes

© Copyright 2016. Laura Sommers.
All rights reserved.
No part of this book may be reproduced in any form or by any electronic or mechanical means without written permission of the author. All text, illustrations and design are the exclusive property of
Laura Sommers
PO Box 33
Phoenix, Maryland 21131

Dedicated to my family.

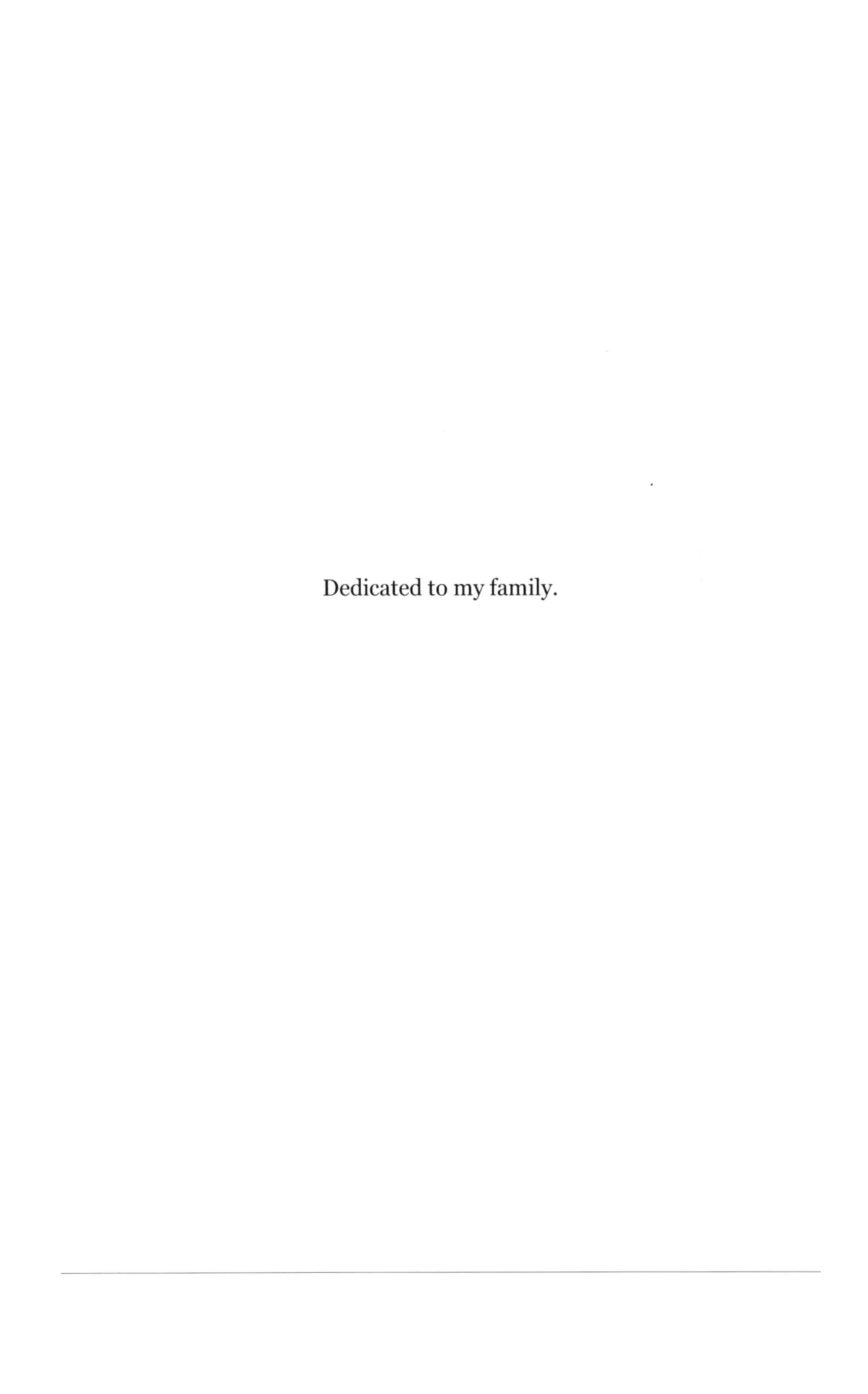

Introduction	i
Memphis Style Coleslaw	1
Tennessee Mud	2
Tennessee Whiskey Balls	3
Memphis Dry Rib Rub	4
Mississippi Delta Baked Chicken	5
Tennessee Cornbread	6
Tennessee Cornbread Salad	7
Memphis Baked Beans	8
Memphis Style Wet Barbecue Sauce	10
Tennessee Icebox Cookies	11
Memphis Sausage and Cheese Platter	12
Southern Fried Chicken	13
Memphis Fried Pork Chops	14
Memphis Country Ham and Red-Eye Gravy	15
Memphis Barbecue Shrimp Chili	16
Beale Street Fried Chitterlings (Chitlins)	17
Memphis Red-Eye Gravy	18
Elvis Presley Peanut Butter Banana and Bacon Sandwich	19
Elvis Presley Blue Hawaiian Cocktail	20
Elvis Presley Clam Bake	21
Shelby County Southern Fried Green Tomatoes	22
Southern Fried Catfish	23
Southern Remoulade Sauce	24
Mid-South Hush Puppies	25
Memphis Style Pizza	26

Memphis Style Barbecue Spaghetti	27
Beale Street Buttermilk Biscuits	28
Roast Beef Memphis Melt	29
Memphis Pork Butt on a Stick	30
Memphis Pulled Pork Nachos	31
Memphis Pulled Pork Sandwich	32
Memphis Barbecue Smoked Ribs with Dry Rub	34
About the Author	37
Other books by Laura Sommers	38

Introduction

Memphis, Tennessee is more than just Elvis Presley and Barbecue Ribs. Memphis is part of Shelby County Tennessee and sits on the Mississippi River as part of the Mississippi Delta on a bluff (high ground) called a "Chickasaw Bluff."

The cuisine consists of its own distinct version of BBQ along with blends of Southern styles and Soul Food. Celebrities such as Elvis Presley, Al and Tipper Gore and Tennessee Ernie Ford have also made their own contributions to the Memphis Style cuisine. Memphis style barbecue is one of the top four styles of barbecue popular in the United States, the other three being Carolina, Kansas City and Texas. The Memphis style of barbecue is distinguished by using pork that has been smoked in a smoker over a long period of time: usually several hours. The sauce is typically a dry rub for the ribs but wet sauce is also used for sandwiches and other nontraditional dishes such as pizza, spaghetti and nachos.

Memphis holds an annual Barbecue Festival on the banks of the Mississippi River blocks away from Beale Street.

Beale Street is a touristy street in the heart of Memphis that is a lot like a mini Bourbon Street in New Orleans, Louisiana. There are many restaurants and pubs located along Beale Street including the famous Rendezvous and Peabody Hotel where trained ducks come down the elevator every morning to festive music while a red carpet is rolled out to lead them to the large fountain in the lobby. The red carpet is again rolled out for them to go back to the elevator and led to the roof of the hotel where they are kept at night.

I lived in Memphis for over three years and spent lots of time studying the culture and cuisine there. I took cooking classes and learned much from the locals what the traditional dishes are that truly represent Memphis style cooking. It was inevitable that I would put together this book with all the recipes gathered from my time there. I hope that you enjoy!

Memphis Style Coleslaw

Ingredients:

1 head green cabbage, tough leaves removed, cored, and shredded
2 carrots, peeled and grated
1 green bell pepper, stemmed, seeded, and finely diced
2 tbsps. grated onion
2 cups mayonnaise
3/4 cup sugar
1/4 cup Dijon mustard
1/4 cup cider vinegar
2 tbsps. celery seeds
1 tsp. salt
1/8 tsp. freshly ground white pepper

Directions:

1. Put cabbage, carrots, bell pepper, and onion in large bowl.
2. Toss thoroughly and set aside.
3. Mix all of the remaining ingredients in another bowl.
4. Pour over vegetables.
5. Toss well to coat.
6. Refrigerate, covered, at least 3 hours.
7. Bring to room temperature before serving.

Tennessee Mud

Ingredients:

1/2 ounce amaretto
1/2 ounce whiskey
5 ounces hot coffee
Whipped cream

Directions:

1. Combine amaretto, whiskey and coffee in coffee mug.
2. Garnish with whipping cream.

Tennessee Whiskey Balls

Ingredients:

2 cups chopped pecans, toasted
1 box (12 ounce size) vanilla wafers, finely crushed
2 cups powdered sugar, plus extra
1/2 cup baking cocoa
1/4 cup corn syrup
1/3 cup whiskey

Directions:

1. Combine all ingredients in a large bowl.
2. Blend well with hands to form and roll into 1 inch balls.
3. Roll balls in powdered sugar.
4. Serve and enjoy!

Memphis Dry Rib Rub

One thing that Memphis is known for is barbeque. There is a barbeque festival held every year on the banks of the Mississippi River blocks away from Beale Street. Memphis Style barbecue is smoked pork that is smothered in this dry rub.

Ingredients:

3 tbsps. paprika
1 tbsp. onion powder
1 tbsp. garlic powder
1 tbsp. dried basil
1 1/2 tbsp. dry mustard
1 tbsp. red pepper
1/2 tbsp. black pepper

Directions:

1. Combine dry rub ingredients and rub onto ribs.
2. Cook ribs over hickory coals at 190 to 200 degrees F for 4 to 5 hours.
3. See recipe later in this book for more detailed instructions on smoking Memphis Style Barbecue Ribs.

Mississippi Delta Baked Chicken

Ingredients:

2 broiler chickens, cut in pieces
6 medium white potatoes, peeled and cubed
8 slices bacon
2 large white onions, chopped
6 large carrots, cubed

Directions:

1. In a heavy duty skillet place a small amount of vegetable oil and brown chicken on all sides.
2. Layer the potatoes, carrots and chopped onions on top of the chicken and lay the bacon strips close together on top of the vegetables.
3. Cover pot and bake at 350 degrees F for 1-1/2 hours.
4. Remove lid from pot and bake an additional 15 minutes.

Tennessee Cornbread

Ingredients:

1/4 cup mild vegetable oil
1/2 cup self-rising flour
1 1/2 cup stone-ground yellow cornmeal
1 tsp. baking powder
1/2 tsp. baking soda
1/2 tsp. salt
3 eggs
2 cups buttermilk

Directions:

1. Preheat oven to 500 degrees F.
2. Place half of the oil in a 12-inch cast-iron skillet and the other half in a large bowl. Place skillet on the stove, over medium heat.
3. Combine flour, cornmeal, baking powder, baking soda and salt in a medium bowl, stir together and set aside.
4. To the oil in the large bowl, add eggs and beat well. Add buttermilk and stir in the dry mixture until nearly smooth. The batter will be thinner than usual for cornbread, more like pancake batter.
5. Pour batter into hot oiled skillet and pop into the oven.
6. Bake until it is brown and crusty, 15 to 20 minutes.

Tennessee Cornbread Salad

Ingredients:

1 package (6 ounce size) buttermilk cornbread mix
12 slices bacon
3 cups chopped tomatoes
1 cup chopped green bell pepper
1 cup chopped onion
1/2 cup chopped sweet pickles, RESERVING
1/4 cup pickle brine
1 cup mayonnaise

Directions:

1. Prepare and bake cornbread as directed on package.
2. Cool completely.
3. In large skillet, cook bacon over medium heat until crisp. Drain on paper towels. Crumble. Crumble half of cornbread into bottom of large serving bowl.
4. In another bowl, combine tomatoes, bell pepper, onions, pickles, and crumbled bacon; mix well. Spoon half of vegetable mixture over cornbread.
5. In small bowl, combine mayonnaise and reserved pickle liquid; mix well. Spread half of mixture over vegetables. Repeat layering with remaining cornbread, vegetables and dressing.
6. Cover tightly; refrigerate 2 to 3 hours before serving.

Memphis Baked Beans

Ingredients:

1 tablespoon olive oil
1 red bell pepper, chopped
1/2 onion, chopped
2 cloves garlic, chopped
2 (28-ounce) cans baked beans
1/2 cup brown sugar
1/3 cup Memphis Dry Rib Rub seasoning (see recipe in book)
1/4 cup molasses
1 cup Memphis wet barbecue sauce (see recipe in book)
3/4 cup pulled pork

Directions:

Preheat oven to 275 degrees F.
In a large Dutch oven, heat oil over medium heat.
Saute the red pepper, onion and garlic until softened, about 2 minutes.
Add the baked beans and remaining ingredients and bring to a low simmer.
Cover the beans and place in the preheated oven.
Bake for 45 minutes.
Serve and enjoy!

Tennessee Ernie Ford's Pea Picking Cake

Ingredients:

1 box (18.25 oz. size) yellow or white cake mix
1/2 cup butter or margarine
4 eggs
1 small can mandarin oranges, (juice reserved)

Frosting:

1 container non-dairy whipped topping
1 small can crushed pineapple (juice reserved)
1 pkg. (3 oz.) instant vanilla pudding mix

Cake Directions:

1. Preheat oven to 350 degrees F.
2. Grease and flour a 9 x 13 inch pan.
3. Combine cake ingredients including oranges in juice.
4. Pour in pan.
5. Bake 35 to 40 minutes in preheated oven.
6. Test cake for doneness with a wooden toothpick inserted in the center that comes out clean.
7. Cool cake before frosting.

Frosting Directions:

8. Combine dry pudding, non-dairy whipped topping and crushed pineapple.
9. Pour reserved pineapple juice over cooled cake.
10. Spread frosting over cake with a spatula.
11. Serve and enjoy!

Memphis Style Wet Barbecue Sauce

Although the Dry Rub is the preferred seasoning for barbecue, Memphians include a wet barbecue sauce to be used for seasonings, dips and the "mop" during the barbecuing process. Even the ribs are first basted with the wet sauce to help the dry rub to stick to the ribs. A traditional recipe for this barbecue sauce is included below.

Ingredients:

2 cups light brown sugar
3 tbsps. ground dry mustard
2 tbsps. ground black pepper
2 tbsps. cayenne pepper
4 cups apple cider vinegar
1 cup vegetable oil
3 tbsps. tomato paste
1 cup ketchup
1 can (28 ounce size) tomato sauce
1 cup grape juice
1/2 cup Worcestershire sauce
3 lemons, washed, quartered, and seeded

Directions:

1. To an unheated, large saucepan or stockpot add dry ingredients. Slowly add vinegar, whisking all of the dry into a paste. Add all other ingredients.
2. Put pan over medium-high heat. Stirring frequently, bring sauce to a boil. Reduce heat and let simmer, uncovered, stirring occasionally, for at least two hours.
3. Move sauce from heat. Remove lemons with a slotted spoon. Let sauce cool for 5-10. Pour warm sauce into a blender or food processor. Pulse on for about 30 seconds. This will keep your sauce from breaking in the refrigerator.
4. Pour the finished sauce into containers and store in refrigerator until you are ready to use. It will keep in the refrigerator for up to six months.

Tennessee Icebox Cookies

Ingredients:

3 cups all-purpose flour
1 tsp. baking soda
1/4 tsp. salt
1 cup unsalted butter, softened
2 1/2 cups firmly packed light brown sugar
1 tbsp. vanilla extract
2 large eggs
1 cup coarsely chopped slivered almonds

Directions:

1. Combine well flour, soda, and salt.
2. Beat butter and brown sugar with an electric mixer about 1 minute until well mixed.
3. Beat in vanilla.
4. Beat in eggs, one at a time, until smooth.
5. Beat in flour mixture well.
6. Add almonds well.
7. Shape dough into 2 inch cylinders about 10 inches long on parchment paper.
8. Chill dough for several hours.
9. Preheat oven to 350 degrees F.
10. Slice cookies 1/4 inch thick.
11. Bake 1 inch apart on cookie sheets for 12 to 15 minutes.
12. Allow to cool on a wire rack.
13. Serve and enjoy.

Memphis Sausage and Cheese Platter

Ingredients:

Links of smoked sausage or kielbasa
1-2 cups Memphis wet barbecue sauce
Memphis dry rub
Sharp cheddar cheese block to cut into cubes

Directions:

1. Heat grill until very hot.
2. Place your sausage on a tray.
3. Dab with BBQ sauce.
4. Sprinkle with barbecue rub.
5. Place sausage on the grill, sauced side down.
6. Put more sauce on side facing up.
7. Sprinkle again with rub.
8. Cook until done.
9. Slice it into pieces about 1/2" thick.
10. Lay on a serving tray.
11. Add cheddar cheese cubes all around sausage.
12. Sprinkle more rub all over – everything, cheese and sausage.
13. Use toothpicks for serving.
14. Serve and enjoy!

Southern Fried Chicken

Ingredients:

3 1/2 lb. chicken, washed and cut into 8 pieces
   1 qt. buttermilk
3 cups flour
2 tsp. paprika
1 tsp. cayenne pepper
2 tsp. salt
1 tsp. freshly ground black pepper
Peanut oil

Directions:

1. Place chicken in a nonreactive pan and add buttermilk.
2. Cover and refrigerate for at least 2 hours or as long as overnight. 2.
3. Combine flour, paprika, cayenne pepper, salt, and black pepper in a large plastic bag, and shake to mix. 3. Heat 3/4" peanut oil in a cast-iron skillet over medium-high heat. 4. Meanwhile, shake each piece of chicken in bag of seasoned flour until well coated. When oil is very hot but not smoking, add chicken, largest pieces first, skin side down. (Work in batches if your skillet is small.) Reduce heat to medium, and cook, turning once, until chicken is golden brown and crispy, 12-15 minutes per side. Drain chicken on paper towels.

Memphis Fried Pork Chops

Ingredients:

1 tsp. seasoned salt, plus more for seasoning
1 tsp. ground black pepper, plus more for seasoning
8 pork breakfast chops
1 cup all-purpose flour
Cayenne pepper
1/2 cup canola oil
1 tbsp. butter

Directions:

1. Watch how to make this recipe.
2. Salt and pepper both sides of the pork chops.
3. Combine the flour and some cayenne, salt and black pepper. Dredge each side of the pork chops in the flour mixture, and then set aside on a plate.
4. Heat the canola oil over medium to medium-high heat.
5. Add butter.
6. When the butter is melted and the butter/oil mixture is hot, cook 3 pork chops at a time, 2 to 3 minutes on the first side.
7. Flip and cook until the chops are golden brown on the other side, 1 to 2 minutes (make sure no pink juices remain).
8. Remove to a plate and repeat with the remaining pork chops.

Memphis Country Ham and Red-Eye Gravy

Ingredients:

Vegetable oil
8 slices thick uncooked country ham
3/4 cup black coffee
1 tsp. sugar
Memphis Red Eye Gravy (recipe below)

Directions:

1. Heat a few drops of oil in a large skillet until skillet is medium hot.
2. Lay ham slices in skillet.
3. Cook on one side for 8.
4. Turn slices and cook for 8 more minutes.
5. Pour coffee into skillet with ham slices. Sprinkle with sugar and stir.
6. Cover and let simmer over very low heat for 5 to 10 minutes.
7. Serve with Memphis Red-Eye Gravy.

Memphis Barbecue Shrimp Chili

Ingredients:

1 1/2 lb. medium shrimp
4 tbsps. unsalted butter
3 tbsps. olive oil
5 cloves garlic, coarsely chopped
1 1/2 cup barbecue sauce
1 tbsp. Worcestershire sauce
1 tsp. hot sauce (Tabasco or similar)
1 tsp. liquid smoke
1 1/2 tsp. crushed red pepper flakes
1 1/2 tsp. salt
1 tsp. freshly ground coarse black pepper
1 tbsp. chili powder
1/2 cup chopped fresh parsley
1 lemon, sliced very thin
White rice, for serving
French bread, for serving

Directions:

1. Peel and clean the shrimp.
2. Melt the butter and oil in a large, heavy skillet.
3. Add the garlic and sauté until soft.
4. Add the shrimp and cook until pink.
5. Add the barbecue, Worcestershire, and hot sauces, the liquid smoke, red pepper flakes, salt, black pepper and chili powder.
6. Simmer 10 minutes.
7. Add the parsley and lemon slices.
8. Simmer 5 to 7 minutes longer.
9. Serve on white rice or with chunks of French bread for dipping.
10. Serve and enjoy!

Beale Street Fried Chitterlings (Chitlins)

Ingredients:

5 lbs. chitterlings
3 quarts water
1 tsp. salt
1/2 tsp. red pepper flakes
1 medium peeled white onions or 1 medium yellow onion
1/4 cup butter

Directions:

1. Put the chitterlings in a large pot along with your 3 quarts water, onion, pepper, and salt.
2. Boil them for 1 1/2 hours or until tender.
3. Add a little extra water if necessary.
4. Prepare a large cast iron skillet with 1/4 stick of butter.
5. Remove chitterlings from pot and slice.
6. Add to the preheated skillet.
7. Stir until lightly brown them.
8. The chitterlings will be done when they are almost falling apart.
9. Serve and enjoy!

Memphis Red-Eye Gravy

Ingredients:

2 slices country ham
1/2 cup brewed coffee or water
2 cups hot cooked grits

Directions:

1. In skillet, cook country ham slices until browned. Remove from skillet. Drain fat, reserving 2 teaspoons.
2. Add the brewed coffee or water to reserved fat. Cook over medium heat for 2 to 3 minutes, stirring in ham drippings from bottom of skillet.
3. Spoon over hot cooked grits and serve with ham slices.

Elvis Presley Peanut Butter Banana and Bacon Sandwich

Ingredients:

3 tbsps. peanut butter
2 slices white bread
1 banana, peeled and sliced
3 slices cooked bacon
1 1/2 tsps. butter

Directions:

1. Spread the peanut butter on one side of one slice of bread.
2. Top with sliced banana, then slices of cooked bacon.
3. Cover with the other slice of bread.
4. Spread butter on the outside of the sandwich.
5. Heat a skillet over medium heat.
6. Fry the sandwich on each side until golden brown and peanut butter is melted, (about 2 minutes on each side).

Elvis Presley Blue Hawaiian Cocktail

Ingredients:

1 fl. oz. light rum 1 fluid ounce blue Curacao liqueur
2 fl. oz. pineapple juice
1 fl. oz. cream of coconut 1 cup crushed ice
1 pineapple slice
1 maraschino cherry

Directions:

1. Combine rum, blue Curacao, pineapple juice, cream of coconut, and 1 cup crushed ice in blender.
2. Puree on high speed until smooth.
3. Pour into chilled highball glass.
4. Garnish with a slice of pineapple and a maraschino cherry.

Elvis Presley Clam Bake

Ingredients:

8 med. red potatoes, scrubbed
1 lb. clams in shell, scrubbed
1 lb. mussels, cleaned and debearded
1/2 lb. unpeeled large shrimp
1 (48 fl. oz.) can chicken broth
1/4 cup dry vermouth
1 1/2 cups butter, divided
1 loaf French bread

Directions:

1. Place a potatoes in a layer in the bottom of a large pot.
2. Cover with a layer of clams, then mussels, and finally the shrimp.
3. Pour in the vermouth and enough chicken broth to fill the pot halfway.
4. Cut a half cup of the butter into cubes and place on top of the seafood.
5. Cover with a lid, and seal tightly with aluminum foil.
6. Bring to a boil, then simmer over medium-low heat for 45 minutes.
7. Remove from the heat, and carefully remove the foil and lid.
8. Remove the seafood and potatoes from the liquid and serve on a large platter.
9. Melt 1/2 cup of reserved butter, and divide into 4 individual dishes for dipping.
10. Serve with French bread.
11. Serve and enjoy!

Shelby County Southern Fried Green Tomatoes

Ingredients:

1 1/2 cups all-purpose flour
1 tsp. ground black pepper
1 tsp. crushed red pepper flakes
1 tsp. garlic powder 2 eggs, lightly beaten
1 (12 fluid ounce) can beer 1/2 cup oil for frying
5 green tomatoes, sliced 1/2 inch thick

Directions:

1. In a bowl, mix the flour, black pepper, red pepper, garlic powder, eggs, and beer.
2. Heat the oil in a skillet over medium heat.
3. Dip tomato slices in the batter to coat.
4. Fry in the skillet 5 minutes on each side, until golden brown.
5. Serve and enjoy!

Southern Fried Catfish

Ingredients:

1 cup yellow cornmeal
1 tbsp. paprika
1 tsp. cayenne pepper
3/4 cup buttermilk
1 tbsp. hot sauce
4 catfish fillets (8-ounces each) skins and bones removed, rinsed and patted dry
Salt and freshly ground black pepper
Peanut oil, for frying
Remoulade Sauce, for dipping, (recipe included)

Directions:

1. Preheat a deep -fryer to 375 degrees F.
2. Mix the cornmeal, paprika and cayenne in a large bowl.
3. In a separate bowl, add the buttermilk and the hot sauce.
4. Season the catfish with salt and pepper.
5. Dredge in the buttermilk and then the cornmeal and spice mixture.
6. Drop carefully in the hot oil.
7. Fry for 4 minutes until crisp.
8. Remove to a paper towel lined sheet tray.
9. Season with salt and pepper.
10. Serve and enjoy!

Southern Remoulade Sauce

Ingredients:

1 cup mayonnaise
1/4 cup Creole mustard
1 tsp. cayenne pepper
1/2 lemon, juiced
1 tbsp. Worcestershire sauce
1 tsp. paprika

Directions:

1. Mix all the ingredients in a small bowl.
2. Serve with Southern Fried Catfish.

Mid-South Hush Puppies

Ingredients:

6 cups peanut oil
1 1/2 cups self-rising cornmeal
1/2 cup self-rising flour
1/2 tsp. baking soda
1/2 tsp. salt
1 small onion, chopped
1 cup buttermilk
1 egg, lightly beaten

Directions:

1. Using a deep pot, preheat oil for frying to 350 degrees F.
2. Stir together the cornmeal, flour, baking soda, and salt in a large bowl.
3. Stir in the onion.
4. In a small bowl, stir together the buttermilk and egg.
5. Pour the buttermilk mixture into the dry ingredients and mix until blended.
6. Drop the batter, 1 teaspoon at a time, into the oil.
7. Dip the spoon in a glass of water after each hushpuppy is dropped in the oil.
8. Fry until golden brown, turning the hushpuppies as they cook.

Memphis Style Pizza

Ingredients:

1/2 cup chopped fresh cilantro
1 cup sliced pepperoncini peppers
1 cup chopped red onion
2 cups shredded Colby-Monterey Jack cheese
1 (12") pre-baked pizza crust
1 cup spicy barbeque sauce
2 skinless boneless chicken breast halves, cooked and cubed

Directions:

1. Preheat oven to 350 degrees F.
2. Place pizza crust on a round pizza baking sheet.
3. Spread the crust with barbeque sauce.
4. Top with chicken, cilantro, pepperoncini peppers, onion, and cheese.
5. Bake in the preheated oven for 15 minutes, or until cheese is melted and bubbly.

Memphis Style Barbecue Spaghetti

Ingredients:

1/2 cup olive oil
2 large onions, diced
1 garlic clove, minced
4 ounces canned diced tomatoes
3 ounces tomato paste
1/4 cup sugar
1 tablespoon fresh oregano, chopped
1 tablespoon fresh basil, chopped
1 cup barbecue sauce
1 1/2 teaspoons kosher salt
16 ounces spaghetti
1 cup pulled pork

Directions:

1. Bring large pot of water to a boil.
2. Pour oil into a large skillet over medium-high heat.
3. When oil shimmers, add onions and garlic.
4. Cook until onion is translucent, stirring often, about 5 minutes.
5. Add diced tomatoes and tomato paste to skillet.
6. Reduce heat to medium-low, and simmer for five minutes.
7. Add sugar, oregano, and basil.
8. Stir well, and cook for another five minutes.
9. Transfer sauce to a blender, and add barbecue sauce.
10. Blend until smooth.
11. Add salt to taste.
12. Add spaghetti to boiling water and cook according to directions on box.
13. Drain pasta when done.
14. Put pasta in a large bowl or the empty pasta pot.
15. Pour in barbecue sauce.
16. Stir well, and add pork.
17. Serve and enjoy!

Beale Street Buttermilk Biscuits

Ingredients:

2 cups flour
4 tsps. baking powder
1/4 tsp. baking soda
3/4 tsp. salt
2 tbsps. butter
2 tbsps. shortening
1 cup buttermilk, chilled

Directions:

1. Preheat oven to 450 degrees F.
2. In a large mixing bowl, combine flour, baking powder, baking soda and salt.
3. Using your fingertips, rub butter and shortening into dry ingredients until mixture looks like crumbs.
4. Make a well in the center and pour in the chilled buttermilk.
5. Stir just until the dough comes together and is very sticky.
6. Turn dough onto floured surface, dust top with flour and gently fold dough over on itself 5 or 6 times.
7. Press into a 1-inch thick round.
8. Cut out biscuits with a 2-inch cutter.
9. Place biscuits on baking sheet so that they just touch. R
10. Reform dough from scrap, working it as little as possible and continue cutting.
11. Bake for 15 to 20 minutes until tall and light brown.

Roast Beef Memphis Melt

Ingredients:

1 Tbsp. Miracle Whip
1 Tbsp. hickory smoke barbecue sauce
1 tsp. yellow mustard
4 slices sourdough bread
8 slices roast beef
1 tomato, cut into 4 slices
2 slices American cheese

Directions:

1. Mix first 3 ingredients in small bowl.
2. Spread bread slices with dressing mixture; fill with remaining ingredients to make 2 sandwiches.
3. Cook in skillet sprayed with cooking spray on medium heat 3 min. on each side or until golden brown on both sides.

Memphis Pork Butt on a Stick

This dish always gets a snicker when served because of the funny name but it is oh so good and served at all fairs and festivals that happen in the Memphis area.
I was quite sad when I left Memphis and could not find this at any carnival or street festival outside of Shelby County, Tennessee. To do it right, you have to use both the dry rub and wet rub. And you have to smoke it, which is how

Ingredients:

1 pork butt or several pounds of pork steaks
Wooden skewers, about 12 inches long
Memphis barbecue dry rub (see recipe)
Memphis wet barbecue sauce (see recipe)

Directions:

1. Cut the pork butt into ¼ inch slices then into strips that are about 2 inches wide.
2. Layer the strips of meat into a bowl and sprinkle my rub onto each layer.
   Sprinkle extra rub on top and cover the bowl.
3. Place the bowl in the fridge overnight to marinate.
4. Soak wooden skewers for several hours.
5. As the sticks are loaded, place them into a Bradley rack with room between each one so the smoke and heat can have ample access.
6. Setup your smoker for cooking at about 225-240 degrees F for about 2 hours and apply smoke for at least 1 hour.
7. Fill smoker water pan ¾ full with water.
8. Add Bradley rack to smoker.
9. When the meat reaches about 170 degrees F, coat both sides with the Wet Barbecue Sauce.
10. You can smoke the meat for 2 or more hours and then transfer the skewers to grill to finish.
11. Keep a spray bottle of water handy to douse any flames if the skewers catch fire.
12. Grill or smoke until meat reaches 225-240 degrees F.
13. Add more sauce as you go.
14. Serve and enjoy!

Memphis Pulled Pork Nachos

Ingredients:

1 (16 oz.) bag tortilla chips
1 lb processed cheese (American, Velveeta, Cheez Whiz), melted
1 cup barbecue sauce
2 lbs barbecued pulled pork
1 four once can pickled jalapeno pepper, drained

Directions:

1. Preheat oven to 400 degrees F.
2. Spread a single layer of tortilla chips on a baking sheet
3. Drizzle with cheese and barbecue sauce and top with a few spoonfuls of meat.
4. Make two more layers the same way.
5. Bake about ten minutes until cheese is bubbly and nachos are heated through.
6. Top with jalapeño slices.

Memphis Pulled Pork Sandwich

Ingredients:

4 lb. boneless pork shoulder with a fat cap
1/4 cup Memphis Dry Rib Rub (recipe included)
Memphis Style Wet Barbecue Sauce (recipe included)
Kaiser rolls or other buns
Memphis Style Coleslaw (recipe included)

Smoker Directions:

1. Rub the pork shoulder with the Memphis Dry Rib Rub.
2. Heat your grill and put meat in a smoker box.
3. Place the shoulder on the unlit side of the grill, fat cap side up.
4. Close the lid and allow it to smoke.
5. Refer to your smoker's instruction manual for more specific directions on smoking the meat.
6. Smoking takes approximately 7 hours to become soft enough to pull apart.
7. During the last hour of cooking, tightly wrap the meat in tinfoil to allow the shoulder to steam in its own moisture.
8. Take the meat off the barbecue and let it stand for 20 minutes.
9. Remove the foil and place the meat in a large stainless steel bowl.
10. Use your hands to break the meat up into tiny pieces.
11. Incorporate all the fat and juices into the meat mixture.

Oven Cooking Directions:

1. Preheat oven 225 degrees F.
2. Rub the pork shoulder liberally with the Memphis Dry Rib Rub.
3. Place the shoulder in a roasting pan, fat cap up, and cook in the preheated oven for 3 and ½ hours.
4. Remove from the oven, wrap with tinfoil, and cook for another 1 and ½ hours to 2 hours.
5. Test for doneness by pushing down on the pork shoulder.
6. It should feel tender and ready to fall apart.
7. Remove from the oven and unwrap the pork.
8. Use two forks to separate the pork while still in the roasting pan.
9. Incorporate drippings and juice back into the pulled pork.

Assembly Directions:

1. Spread rolls with Memphis Style Wet Barbecue Sauce.
2. Lay down pulled pork.
3. Drizzle with more Memphis Style Wet Barbecue Sauce.
4. Add Memphis Style Cole Slaw.
5. Add the top bun.
6. Serve and enjoy!

Memphis Barbecue Smoked Ribs with Dry Rub

Ingredients:

Pork Spare Ribs – 3 racks
Memphis Style Dry Rib Rub (recipe included)
Hickory wood Chunks – soaked in water for smoking
Light brown sugar to prepare meat
Tin Foil
Foil Pan for drip pan
Water

Mop Sauce Ingredients:

1 cup apple juice
1 cup apple cider vinegar
1 tbsp. prepared mustard
1 tbsp. Memphis Style Dry Rib Rub
Mop brush

Preparing the Ribs:

1. Trim off the flap on the bone side of the ribs
2. Trim up the racks of ribs of any excessive fat or connective tissue
3. Trim up the ends of the ribs, squaring them off and trim off any excessive meat with no bone in it from along the bottom side of the rack – this allows the meat to cook more evenly. You can also trim them into St Louise Style ribs if you want. Follow this link and we'll show you how to do it
4. Score the membrane on the bone side of the rack in a cross hatch pattern – this allows the rub to penetrate better. You can also remove it if you would like. We show you how to do this here
5. Place rub on liberally on all sides of each rack of ribs – rub it in to get a good even coating
6. Let the rub set on the ribs for 2 hours in the refrigerator.
7. Place small hardwood chunks in water to soak

Setting Up The Grill:

1. Grill should be set up for indirect grilling: coals on one side of the grill and no coals on the other side.
2. Place a chimney of unlit coals on one side of the grill.
3. Place ½ chimney of lit coals on top of the unlit coals.
4. Place a foil drip pan opposite the unlit coals
5. Pour water into the drip pan to keep the ribs moist.
6. Grill temperature should be between 250 to 300 degrees Fahrenheit.

Mop Sauce Directions:

Mix all the Mop Sauce ingredients together in a bowl.

Cooking Directions:

1. Give the ribs a dusting of light brown sugar on all sides of the rack.
2. Reapply rub on all sides of the rack.
3. Place the ribs bone side down on the side of the grill over the drip pan
4. Place a piece of the soaked hickory wood onto the hot coals.
5. The cooking time will be about 4 hours.
6. Mop the top of the ribs with the mopping sauce after one hour.
7. Mop the top of the ribs with the mopping sauce after two hours.
8. Add another chunk of hardwood to the coals after three hours.
9. Rotate the rack of ribs 180 degrees to ensure even cooking.
10. Mop the top of the ribs with the mopping sauce.
11. Add another chunk of hardwood to the coals
12. Take the rack of ribs off the grill and wrap in tin foil to rest and redistribute the juices.
13. Let rest for 15 minutes to 30 minutes
14. Cut ribs into smaller slabs or pieces for serving.
15. Sprinkle liberally with Memphis Dry Rib Rub.
16. Serve and Enjoy!

The End

About the Author

Laura Sommers is a loving wife and mother who lives on a small farm in Baltimore County, Maryland and has a passion for all things domestic especially when it comes to saving money. She has a profitable eBay business and is a couponing addict. She challenges herself to write books that are enriching, enjoyable, and often unconventional.

Other books by Laura Sommers

- Easy to Make Party Dip Recipes: Chips and Dips and Salsa and Whips!
- Super Slimming Vegan Soup Recipes!
- Popcorn Lovers Recipe Book
- Inexpensive Low Carb Recipes
- Recipes for the Zombie Apocalypse: Cooking Meals with Shelf Stable Foods
- Best Traditional Irish Recipes for St. Patrick's Day
- Egg Recipes for People With Backyard Chickens
- Awesome Sugar Free Diabetic Pie Recipes
- Super Awesome Traditional Maryland Recipes
- Super Awesome Farm Fresh Pork Chop Recipes
- Super Summer Barbecue and Pool Party Picnic Salads!

May all of your meals be a banquet
with good friends and good food.